Lunch

Elizabeth Nonweiler

sals

haggis

wontons

cobb salad

korma

cod and chips

chakalaka

sh and ackee

falafe

tom yum goong

beetroot broth

pasta with mushrooms

Interesting facts about the pictures

page 2: **Salsa** means "sauce" in Spanish, but in English it means a dish from Mexico or South America served with corn chips. It is made with tomatoes, onions and chilli peppers.

page 3: **Haggis** is a Scottish dish made from the liver, heart and lungs of a sheep, mixed with oats and pepper. It tastes good with neeps (turnip or swede) and tatties (mashed potato).

page 4: **Wontons** are Chinese dumplings. A square of dough is spread with ground pork and shrimp and wrapped up to seal in the mixture. Then it is boiled in soup.

page 5: **Cobb salad** is a mixture of lettuce, tomatoes, avocado, eggs, bacon, chicken and cheese, with a salad dressing. It was first eaten in Robert Cobb's restaurant in the United States.

page 6: **Korma** comes from India and Pakistan. It is made with vegetables or meat cooked in a creamy spicy sauce, served with naan bread.

page 7: **Cod and chips** means fish and chips made with cod. The cod is dipped in batter and fried; the chips are made from sliced potatoes and fried. Fish and chips came first from England.

page 8: **Chakalaka** is from South Africa. It is made with onions, peppers, tomatoes and baked beans. It is very spicy, so it is often served with pap, which is a bland cornmeal porridge.

page 9: **Fish and ackee** is from Jamaica. The fish is salted and cooked with ackee, a white fruit that comes from inside a red pod. Fish and ackee may be served with rice and peas.

page 10: **Falafel** comes from the Middle East. It is made by crushing chickpeas with spices, forming them into balls and frying them. This falafel is served with lettuce and yogurt.

page 11: **Tom Yum Goong** is a hot and sour soup from Thailand. It is made with fish stock, lemongrass, lime juice, chilli peppers and other tasty ingredients. This one has shrimps in it.

page 12: **Beetroot broth** is sometimes called borsch and comes from Russia. It is made with beetroot, cabbage, carrots and other vegetables with a blob of sour cream on top.

page 13: **Pasta and mushrooms** have been mixed with cheese to make this dish from Italy. Pasta is made from flour and water and comes in many shapes. These pasta swirls are called fusilli.

Letter-sound correspondences

Level 1 books cover the following letter-sound correspondences. Letter-sound correspondences highlighted in **green** can be found in this book.

ant	big	cat	dog	egg	fish	get	hot	it
jet	key	let	man	nut	off	pan	queen	run
sun	tap	up	van	wet	box	yes	zoo	

duck	fish	chips	sing	thin this	keep	look moon	art	corn